Cool

Gulf Coast Cooking

Easy and Fun
Regional Recipes

Alex Kuskowski

visit us at www.abdopublishing.com

Published by ABDO Publishing Company, a division of ABDO, P.O. Box 398166, Minneapolis, Minnesota 55439. Copyright © 2014 by Abdo Consulting Group, Inc. International copyrights reserved in all countries. No part of this book may be reproduced in any form without written permission from the publisher. Super SandCastle™ is a trademark and logo of ABDO Publishing Company.

Printed in the United States of America, North Mankato, Minnesota
062013
092013

PRINTED ON RECYCLED PAPER

Editor: Liz Salzmann
Content Developer: Nancy Tuminelly
Cover and Interior Design and Production:
Colleen Dolphin, Mighty Media, Inc.
Food Production: Desirée Bussiere
Photo Credits: Colleen Dolphin, Shutterstock

The following manufacturers/names appearing in this book are trademarks: Heinz®, Hillshire Farm®, Kemps®, Lea & Perrins®, Market Pantry™, Nellie & Joe's®, Roundy's®

Library of Congress Cataloging-in-Publication Data

Kuskowski, Alex.
  Cool Gulf Coast cooking : easy and fun regional recipes / Alex Kuskowski.
      pages cm. -- (Cool USA cooking)
  Audience: 8-12.
  Includes index.
  ISBN 978-1-61783-829-3
  1. Cooking, American--Southern style--Juvenile literature.
  2. Cooking--Alabama--Gulf Coast--Juvenile literature.
  I. Title.
  TX715.2.S68K87 2014
  641.5976--dc23
                              2013001891

Safety First!

Some recipes call for activities or ingredients that require caution. If you see these symbols ask an adult for help!

HOT STUFF!
This recipe requires the use of a stove or oven. Always use pot holders when handling hot objects.

SUPER SHARP!
This recipe includes the use of a sharp **utensil** such as a knife or grater.

Cuisine Cooking

Each regional recipe can have a lot of **versions**. Many are **unique** to the cook. The recipes in this book are meant to give you just a taste of regional cooking. If you want to learn more about one kind of cooking, go to your local library or search online. There are many great recipes to try!

Contents

Discover Gulf Coast Eats!

Gulf Coast cooking has tons of flavors for your taste buds to explore! Herbs, vegetables, seafood, and grains are all easy to find in this region. They are used in many cooking **techniques**, from Creole to Cajun to Floribbean.

The Gulf Coast states are the southernmost part of the United States. It is warm and muggy most of the year. That makes it easy to grow crops such as rice, beans, and vegetables. The states all border water too. That means a lot of fish. The **variety** of ingredients helps make Gulf Coast food **unique**.

There is a lot to learn about foods from the Gulf Coast. Use the recipes in this book to have your own feast. Try them all, or make up your own. Grab a chef's hat, it's time for a cooking adventure!

Learn About the Gulf Coast

Regional cooking has a lot to do with where the ingredients and recipes are from. Every region has its own **culture**. What do you know about Gulf Coast culture and food?

Mississippi

Catfish is a very popular food in Mississippi. Many people eat it with balls of fried cornmeal called hushpuppies.

Florida

Florida is known for two things. Fish and fruit. It has about 100 million **citrus** trees and produces 90 million pounds of seafood a year.

Alabama

Barbecue is popular all over the south. Many states have BBQ cook-offs and special recipes.

Louisiana

There are two types of **cuisine** that started in Louisiana. They are Creole and Cajun. Settlers from Spain, Portugal, Italy, and France developed these styles.

Texas

Tex-Mex, short for Texas Mexican, is a clash of cooking cultures. But it makes for some **delicious** meals.

The Basics

Ask Permission

Before you cook, ask **permission** to use the kitchen, cooking tools, and ingredients. If you'd like to do something yourself, say so. Just remember to be safe. If you would like help, ask for it. Always ask for help using a stove or oven.

Be Prepared

- Be organized. Knowing where everything is makes cooking easier and safer.

- Read the directions all the way through before you start. Remember to follow the directions in order.

- The most important ingredient in great cooking is preparation! Set out all your ingredients before starting.

Be Neat and Clean

- Start with clean hands, clean tools, and a clean work surface.

- Tie back long hair so it stays out of the food.

- Wear comfortable clothing. Roll up long sleeves.

Be Smart, Be Safe

- Never work in the kitchen if you are home alone.

- Always have an adult close by for hot jobs, such as using the oven or the stove.

- Have an adult around when using a sharp tool, such as a knife or grater. Always be careful when using them!

- Remember to turn pot handles toward the back of the stove. That way you won't accidentally knock them over.

Cool Cooking Terms

Peel
Peel means to remove the skin, often with a peeler.

Chop
Chop means to cut into small pieces.

Knead
Knead means to press, fold, or stretch something such as bread dough.

Dice/Cube
Dice and *cube* mean to cut something into small squares.

Slice
Slice means to cut food into pieces of the same thickness.

Grate
Grate means to shred something into small pieces using a grater.

Whisk
Whisk means to beat quickly by hand with a whisk or a fork.

Mince
Mince means to cut or chop into very small pieces.

The Tool Box

Here are some of the tools that you'll need for the recipes in this book.

8 × 8-inch baking dish

baking sheet

frying pan

grater

measuring cups & spoons

mixing bowls

mixing spoon

pot holders

rubber spatula

saucepan

slotted spoon

whisk

The Ingredients

Here are some of the ingredients that you'll need for the recipes in this book.

avocado	black olives	buttermilk
canned tomatoes	cayenne pepper	celery
chicken breasts	chicken broth	chili powder
cider vinegar	garlic cloves	graham cracker crust

green pepper

key lime juice

kidney beans

lime

okra

onion

paprika

red pepper

scallions

shrimp

sweetened condensed milk

taco seasoning mix

turkey sausages

white rice

Worcestershire sauce

13

Tex-Mex 7-Layer Bean Dip

Dig into this hearty & delicious snack!

Makes 8 servings

Ingredients

1 15-ounce can refried beans
1 packet taco seasoning mix
1 cup grated Monterey Jack cheese
16 ounces salsa
¼ cup chopped green pepper
1 avocado, peeled and chopped
⅓ cup sour cream
½ cup chopped scallions
½ cup chopped black olives
3 cups tortilla chips

Tools

measuring cups
large saucepan
mixing spoon
large serving dish
grater
sharp knife
cutting board

*hot!
*sharp!

1 Put the refried beans and ¼ cup water in a saucepan. Cook on medium heat. Stir **occasionally**. Remove from heat when the beans begin to bubble.

2 Stir in taco seasoning mix.

3 Spread the beans in the bottom of the serving dish. Sprinkle the cheese on top of the beans.

4 Spread the salsa on top of the cheese. Add the green peppers and avocado. Add spoonfuls of sour cream.

5 Sprinkle the scallions and olives on top. Serve with chips for the perfect snack.

Even Cooler!

Add green chilis for an extra kick!
It's the state pepper of Texas.

New Orleans Beignets

Try this scrumptious Southern doughnut!

Makes 25 beignets

Ingredients

2¾ cups flour
½ cup sugar
2 teaspoons baking powder
½ teaspoon baking soda
½ teaspoon salt
1 cup buttermilk
1 egg
1 teaspoon vanilla extract
3 cups vegetable oil
¼ cup powdered sugar

Tools

*hot!
*sharp!

measuring cups
measuring spoons
medium mixing bowl
large mixing bowl
whisk
sharp knife
large frying pan
fryer thermometer
slotted spoon
paper towels

1 Put the flour, sugar, baking powder, baking soda, and salt in a medium mixing bowl. Stir and set the bowl aside.

2 Put the buttermilk, egg, vanilla extract, and ⅓ cup water in a large mixing bowl. Whisk well. Add the flour mixture to the buttermilk mixture. Stir until doughy.

3 Sprinkle flour on a clean work surface. Place the dough on the flour. Sprinkle flour on your hands. Lightly knead the dough. Flatten the dough into a square. Cover a knife with flour. Cut the dough into 2-inch (5 cm) squares.

4 Put the vegetable oil in a large frying pan. Heat the oil to 325 degrees. Use a slotted spoon to lower the dough squares into the oil.

5 Cook one side for 3 minutes. Use the spoon to flip them over. Cook for another 3 minutes.

6 Use the slotted spoon to remove the beignets. Put them on paper towels. Sprinkle powdered sugar on top.

Cajun Spiced Pretzels

Serve your friends this spicy snack!

Makes 5 servings

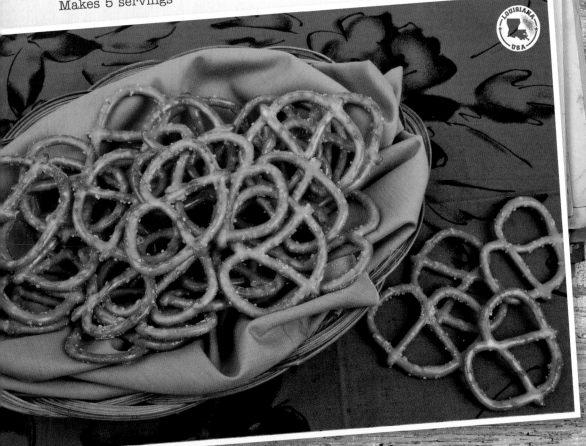

Ingredients

½ cup vegetable oil
½ ounce ranch salad dressing mix
½ teaspoon garlic salt
½ teaspoon cayenne pepper
½ teaspoon onion powder
3½ cups pretzel twists

Tools

measuring cups
measuring spoons
large mixing bowl
mixing spoon
baking sheet
pot holders

*hot!

1 Preheat the oven to 200 degrees.

2 Put the vegetable oil, dressing mix, garlic salt, cayenne pepper, and onion powder in a large bowl. Stir.

3 Add the pretzels. Use your hands to toss the pretzels. Make sure they get coated with the oil mixture.

4 Put the pretzels on the baking sheet. Bake for 80 minutes. Take them out every 30 minutes to stir them.

5 When the pretzels are finished baking, let them cool. Then chow down on this tasty snack!

Tip: Try using mini pretzels.

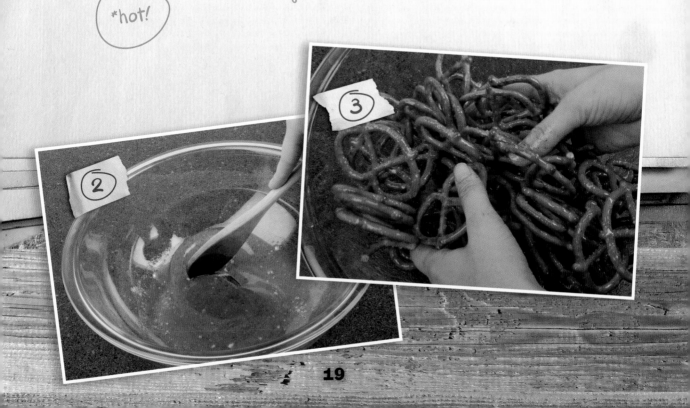

19

Gulf Coast Gumbo

Make this soup an everyday favorite!

Makes 5 servings

Ingredients

2 tablespoons butter
¼ cup flour
1 green pepper, chopped
1 onion, chopped
3 stalks celery, chopped
2 cups chicken broth
6 tomatoes, diced
2 teaspoons Worcestershire sauce
½ teaspoon thyme
3 garlic cloves, minced
½ cup parsley
½ teaspoon salt
½ teaspoon black pepper
½ cayenne pepper
1 pound shrimp, peeled

Tools

large saucepan with cover
measuring cups & spoons
mixing spoon
sharp knife
cutting board
pot holders

*hot!
*sharp!

1   Melt the butter in a large saucepan over medium heat. Stir in the flour. The flour will turn brown and become thicker. Cook for 10 minutes. Turn the heat to low.

2   Add the green pepper, onion, and celery. Stir and cook 15 minutes.

3   Add the chicken broth. Turn the heat to medium.

4   Cook until the broth begins to boil. Stir in the tomatoes, Worcestershire sauce, thyme, garlic, parsley, salt, black pepper, and cayenne pepper.

5   Turn the heat down to low. Cover the pan. Cook 20 minutes.

6   Add the shrimp and stir. Cook 10 minutes. Serve warm.

By the Sea Beans and Rice

A tasty side dish or a meal all by itself!

Makes 6 servings

Ingredients

¼ cup vegetable oil
1 cup chopped onion
1 green pepper, chopped
2 garlic cloves, minced
1 can (15.25 ounces) kidney beans
1 teaspoon salt
1 teaspoon cayenne pepper
2 teaspoons dried oregano
2 turkey sausages, sliced
1½ cup white rice

Tools

measuring cups
large saucepan with cover
mixing spoon
sharp knife
cutting board
measuring spoons
medium saucepan
pot holders

*hot!
*sharp!

1. Heat the oil in large saucepan for 30 seconds. Stir in the onion, green pepper, and garlic.

2. Cook for 5 minutes on medium heat, or until the onions turn clear.

3. Add 6 cups water and the beans. Add the salt, cayenne pepper, and oregano. Stir everything together. Cover the pan. Cook on medium-low heat for 2 hours.

4. Stir in sausages. Put the lid back on and cook for another 30 minutes.

5. Put the rice and 3 cups water in a medium saucepan. Bring water to a boil. Turn down the heat. Let it simmer for 20 minutes. Serve the beans over the rice!

Creole Cooked Okra & Tomatoes

A tasty side dish to go with any meal!

Makes 5 servings

Ingredients

3 cups chopped okra

1 cup chopped onion

1 cup chopped red pepper

¾ cup canned tomatoes, chopped

5 tablespoons vegetable oil

1 teaspoon basil

1 teaspoon chopped scallions

1½ tablespoons salt

¼ teaspoon cayenne pepper

¼ teaspoon black pepper

½ teaspoon dried thyme

½ teaspoon dried oregano

1 tablespoon minced garlic

Tools

sharp knife

cutting board

measuring cups

measuring spoons

large mixing bowl

mixing spoon

8 × 8-inch baking dish

aluminum foil

pot holders

1   Preheat the oven to 300 degrees.

2   Put all ingredients in a large mixing bowl. Stir well. Make sure the okra gets coated with the oil and seasonings.

3   Put the mixture in the baking dish. Cover it with aluminum foil.

4   Bake 90 minutes. Stir the mixture once every 30 minutes while baking.

5   Remove aluminum foil for the last 15 minutes of baking time. Take it out of the oven. Serve as a super side dish that adds **pizzazz** to any meal!

*hot!
*sharp!

Sweet Home Spicy BBQ

Serve up some bold flavor!

Makes 4 servings

Ingredients

4 boneless, skinless
 chicken breast halves
1½ tablespoons sugar
½ tablespoon paprika
½ teaspoon salt
½ teaspoon dry mustard
¼ teaspoon chili powder
⅛ cup cider vinegar
⅛ teaspoon cayenne pepper
1 tablespoon Worcestershire
 sauce
¾ cup tomato-vegetable juice
¼ cup ketchup
1 clove garlic, minced

Tools

9 × 13-inch baking dish
measuring cups & spoons
medium mixing bowl
mixing spoon
pot holders
fork
tongs
cutting board

*hot!

1   Preheat the oven to 350 degrees.

2   Arrange the chicken in the baking dish.

3   Put the remaining ingredients in the mixing bowl.
Add 1 tablespoon water. Stir until completely mixed.

4   Pour the mixture over the chicken. Bake for 35 minutes.

5   Take the chicken out of the oven. Use tongs and a fork
to shred the chicken breasts. Put the chicken back in the
baking dish.

6   Stir to cover the shredded chicken with sauce. Bake
another 10 minutes. Take it out and let it cool. Have a
taste of this **delicious** dish!

Tang-a-licious Key Lime Pie

This simple and sweet pie has a bite!

Makes 8 servings

Ingredients

14 ounces sweetened
  condensed milk
2 eggs
1 cup key lime juice
9-inch graham cracker crust
1 cup whipped topping
1 lime, sliced

Tools

measuring cups
measuring spoons
large mixing bowl
whisk
rubber spatula
pot holders
sharp knife
cutting board

*hot!
*sharp!

1   Preheat the oven to 350 degrees.

2   Put the condensed milk, eggs, and key lime juice in the mixing bowl. Whisk until smooth.

③   Pour the mixture into the pie crust. Fill the crust completely. Bake for 15 minutes.

④   Refrigerate for 2 hours. Spread on the whipped topping.

5   When ready to serve, **garnish** each piece with lime slices. Serve up a sweet and sour classic!

Conclusion

Now you know how to make some wonderful Gulf Coast dishes! Did you learn anything about Cajun **cuisine**? Did you try any new Creole foods? Everywhere you go there are new foods to experience.

From coast to coast the United States is a land of **delicious** dishes! East Coast, Pacific Coast, Gulf Coast, Midwest, South, and West are the main regions of US cuisine. Try them all to get a taste of the United States. See if one is your favorite!

Glossary

citrus – a fruit such as an orange, lemon, or lime that has a thick skin and a juicy pulp.

cuisine – a style of preparing and presenting food.

culture – the behavior, beliefs, art, and other products of a particular group of people.

delicious – very pleasing to taste or smell.

garnish – to decorate with small amounts of food.

occasionally – sometimes, once in a while, or from time to time.

permission – when a person in charge says it's okay to do something.

pizzazz – the quality of being exciting or attractive.

technique – a method or style in which something is done.

unique – different, unusual, or special.

utensil – a tool used to prepare or eat food.

variety – different types of one thing.

version – a different form or type from the original.

Web Sites

To learn more about regional US cooking, visit ABDO Publishing Company online at www.abdopublishing.com. Web sites about easy and fun regional recipes are featured on our Book Links page. These links are routinely monitored and updated to provide the most current information available.

Index